Industrialization in America

By
MARIA BACKUS

D1566840

COPYRIGHT © 2002 Mark Twain Media, Inc.

ISBN 1-58037-184-1

Printing No. CD-1530

Mark Twain Media, Inc., Publishers
Distributed by Carson-Dellosa Publishing Company, Inc.

Table of Contents

About the American History Series

Welcome to *Industrialization in America*, one of the books in the Mark Twain Media, Inc., American History series for students in grades four to seven.

The activity books in this series are designed as stand-alone material for classrooms and home-schoolers or as supplemental material to enhance your history curriculum. Students can be encouraged to use the books as independent study units to improve their understanding of historical events and people.

Each book provides challenging activities that enable students to explore history, geography, and social studies topics. The activities provide research opportunities and promote critical reading, thinking, and writing skills. As students follow the contributions of famous inventors and how the Industrial Revolution changed history, they will draw conclusions; write opinions; compare and contrast historical events, people, and places; analyze cause and effect; and improve mapping skills. Students will also have the opportunity to apply what they learn to their own lives through reflection and creative writing.

Students can further increase their knowledge and understanding of historical events by using reference sources at the library and on the Internet. Students may need assistance to learn how to use search engines and discover appropriate websites.

Titles of books for additional reading appropriate to the subject matter at this grade level are included in each book.

Although many of the questions are open-ended, answer keys are included at the back of the book for questions with specific answers.

Share a journey through history with your students as you explore the books in the Mark Twain Media, Inc., American History series:

Discovering and Exploring the Americas
Life in the Colonies
The American Revolution
The Lewis and Clark Expedition
The Westward Movement
The California Gold Rush
The Oregon and Santa Fe Trails
Slavery in the United States
The American Civil War
Abraham Lincoln and His Times
The Reconstruction Era
Industrialization in America
The Roaring Twenties and Great Depression
World War II and the Post-war Years
America in the 1960s and 1970s
America in the 1980s and 1990s

Industrialization Time Line

1698   Thomas Savery builds a steam engine that can pump water out of flooded mines.

1712   Thomas Newcomen builds his first steam engine.

1764   James Hargreaves develops the spinning jenny.

1764   James Watt invents a separate condenser steam engine.

1782   James Watt builds a steam engine that can produce rotary motion.

1793   Samuel Slater opens the first working U.S. cotton mill.

1793   Eli Whitney invents the cotton gin.

1797   Eli Whitney contracts to make 10,000 muskets for the U.S. Army using interchangeable parts and mass production methods.

1804   Richard Trevithick builds the first steam locomotive that can run on rails.

1807   Robert Fulton's steamboat, the *Clermont*, travels between New York City and Albany.

1817   Work begins on the Erie Canal.

1825   The Erie Canal is completed.

1829   George Stephenson builds the *Rocket,* a steam locomotive that can reach 30 mph.

1831   Michael Faraday invents the dynamo, an early type of electric generator.

1837   Samuel Morse invents the magnetic telegraph.

1844   Samuel Morse sends a message by telegraph from Washington, D.C. to Baltimore.

1850   Isaac Singer produces the first successful sewing machine.

1851   The Great Exhibition in London becomes the model for all World's Fairs to come.

1851   The Bessemer steel-making process is developed.

1857   A New York department store installs the first safety elevator.

1859   The first oil well is drilled.

1862   Louis Pasteur shows how germs cause disease.

1868   Christopher Sholes invents the first practical typewriter.

1868   George Westinghouse invents air brakes for trains.

1869   The first transcontinental railway is completed in the United States.

1876   Alexander Graham Bell invents the telephone.

1877   Thomas Edison invents the phonograph.

1879   Thomas Edison perfects an incandescent light bulb.

1885   Karl Benz builds one of the first gasoline-powered automobiles.

1885   The first skyscraper is built in Chicago.

1888   Heinrich Hertz discovers radio waves.

1888   George Eastman introduces a hand-held box camera for portable use.

1901   Guglielmo Marconi sends radio waves across the Atlantic Ocean.

1903   The Wright Brothers make the first successful airplane.

1908   The first Model T Ford is built.

Name: _____ Date: _____

Industrialization

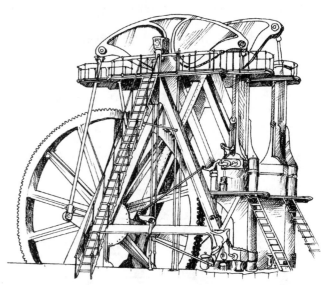

The word *industrialization* refers to the process of using **power-driven** machinery to manufacture goods. Industrialization has provided tremendous benefits for people, but it has also created great hardships, especially in the past. You will be learning about the many aspects of industrialization in this book.

For hundreds of years, people used muscle power, wind power, and water power to help them in their daily work. Most people depended on the land to grow food or raise sheep and cattle. Then, during the 1700s, people in Britain began to find better ways to farm, to make cloth and metals, and to transport people and goods. In 1782, James Watt, a Scottish engineer, perfected the **steam engine**. Steam engines, which were fueled by coal, provided the first reliable source of power. Manufacturers soon put steam engines to work running all sorts of machinery.

Once steam engines were available, people no longer depended on the land. More people left their small family farms and moved to cities to work in industry. There was so much industrialization going on during the 1700s and the 1800s that this time period is sometimes called the **Industrial Revolution**.

The word *revolution* makes it sound like there was a very sudden change. That's not true. The changeover from human power to machine power had been going on very gradually for 200 years before the Industrial Revolution. All the changes that occurred during the Industrial Revolution were due to the ideas and discoveries of people who had lived long before that time.

The Industrial Revolution started in Britain. Then it spread to the rest of Europe, the United States, and the rest of the world. If you think about it, you will realize that industrialization continues right into our present time.

Answer the following questions. Use your own paper if you need more room.

1. What types of power did people depend upon before steam engines were available?

   _____

2. Why was a steam engine a reliable source of power? _____

   _____

3. The word *revolution* gives the idea of a sudden change. Did the Industrial Revolution start up in a specific year? Explain your answer on your own paper.

4. How does industrialization continue into our present time? Explain your answer on your own paper.

Name: _____   Date: _____

What Is a Machine?

Answer the questions below. Use your own paper if you need more room.

1. What is a machine? Use your own words to write a definition. _____

   _____

2. List six machines that you have in your home. _____

   _____

3. Which one would you most *not* want to part with? Why not? _____

   _____

   _____

4. How do these machines make your life easier? _____

   _____

   _____

5. How could machines make people's lives more complicated? _____

   _____

   _____

6. Thousands of years ago, people invented simple machines that made lifting and moving heavy loads much easier. The ancient Egyptians used levers and wedges to build the pyramids. In the Middle Ages, people used pulleys to construct the towers on cathedrals. These early machines made work much easier, but they still required manual labor, that is, human muscle power. What machines do you have in your home that require some "muscle power"?

   _____

   _____

7. Before 1700, most people in Europe lived in rural areas and used homemade products. Although there were a few simple factories where people worked together to make luxury items, such as cloth laced with gold thread, there was little industry. What does *industry* mean?

   _____

8. Besides their own muscle power and animal power, people had two other power sources: water and wind. How can wind be a source of power? How could water be a source of power?

   _____

   _____

Name: _____ Date: _____

Water Power

Waterwheels were used in Europe for hundreds of years to grind grain, pound rags to make paper, drive hammers for metalworking, power saws, tan leather, treat cloth, and hoist stone and coal from quarries and mines.

During the 1700s, thousands of water-powered mills were also built in America. These mills were used to saw logs into lumber, to clean homespun wool fabric, and to do many other jobs.

There were several types of waterwheels. One type was called the **overshot wheel**. Water from the stream or river was brought to the top of the wheel by a flume or sluice. The water filled the "buckets" that were attached to the wheel. The weight of the water in the buckets pushed the wheel downwards. The buckets emptied out at the bottom and returned to the top empty. The buckets filling and emptying kept the wheel rotating. The center of the wheel was attached to one end of a shaft. The other end of the shaft was attached to gears.

In the picture below, the gears are attached to two grinding stones. Wheat or oats could be dumped into the top of the grinding stones. The motion of the grinding stones would crush the grain into flour. The flour would come out near the bottom of the grinding stones and be put into bags.

Look at the illustration below. Write the words from the box on the correct lines.

stream	**shaft**	**sluice**	**buckets**
gears	**flour**	**wheel**	**grinding stones**

A. _____   D. _____

E. _____

F. _____

B. _____

G. _____

H. _____

C. _____

Name: _____ Date: _____

Inventions

One of the reasons why industrialization occurred was that there were so many new inventions. Competitions with prizes were even set up to encourage inventors.

Answer each question below. You may work with a partner. Then share your ideas with your classmates.

1. What does it mean to *invent* something? _____

   _____

   _____

2. Why do you think people invent things? _____

   _____

   _____

3. A well-known saying is "Necessity is the mother of invention." What do you think this saying means?

   _____

   _____

   _____

4. Do inventions just "spring out" of people's heads, or are they more likely a result of improvements to other inventions? Give examples to support your ideas.

   _____

   _____

   _____

   _____

5. Circle the qualities that an inventor needs.

   observant   curious   resourceful   clever   intelligent   patient

6. In your opinion, are there other qualities that are more important? What are the two most important qualities for an inventor?

   _____

   _____

   _____

6

Name: _____ Date: _____

Your Invention

Answer the questions below. Use your own paper if you need more room.

1. If you were to invent something, what would it be? _____

   _____

   _____

2. What would your invention do? _____

   _____

   _____

3. What would you call your invention? _____

   _____

   _____

4. How would your invention improve your life or another person's life? _____

   _____

   _____

5. How does your invention draw upon other inventions? What has to be invented before you can invent your item?

   _____

   _____

   _____

6. Draw a picture of your invention in the picture frame below. Label the parts of your invention.

Name: _____ Date: _____

Standardized Parts

Answer the questions below. Use your own paper if you need more room.

1. What have you made that is unique, something that is unlike anything else in the world?

   _____

   _____

2. Why is making something that is unique a satisfying experience? _____

   _____

   _____

3. Although it is satisfying to own or make unique things, what would happen if your family's car was slightly different from every other make or model of the same car? How would you replace a faulty steering column or a broken headlight?

   _____

   _____

4. For things like cars and computers, *uniformity* makes parts *interchangeable.* Use a dictionary to look up the words and write the definitions on the lines below.

   Define *uniformity.* _____

   Define *interchangeable.* _____

5. Eli Whitney was the nineteenth-century inventor who first put into practice the idea of standardized parts. Standardized parts are all made exactly the same. Before his time, everything was made individually. Each item was slightly different from every other item of its kind. How do you think standardized parts influenced American manufacturing?

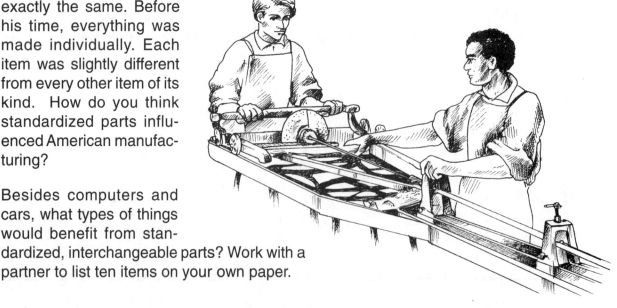

6. Besides computers and cars, what types of things would benefit from standardized, interchangeable parts? Work with a partner to list ten items on your own paper.

Name: _____ Date: _____

Eli Whitney's Solutions

Read the paragraphs below. Fill in the problems and solutions on the lines below.

In 1797, the United States feared it might soon be at war with France, so the government wanted to obtain 40,000 muskets. Fortunately, the war did not happen. This event, however, inspired Eli Whitney to find a way to manufacture guns more efficiently. Before that time, each gun was individually made by a skilled gunsmith. If a part broke, the replacement part had to be custom-made for that gun. Whitney realized that if each gun had interchangeable parts, then it would be easy to replace broken parts.

Problem #1: Replacement parts for guns had to be custom-made.

Eli Whitney's Solution: _____

_____

There was a shortage of skilled gunsmiths in the country at the time. Whitney designed the kind of machines that could be run by unskilled workers.

Problem #2: _____

Eli Whitney's Solution: _____

_____

Eli Whitney set up a gun factory in 1798. He wanted to produce 10,000 muskets for the U.S. government. Some people didn't think his idea of interchangeable parts would work. Whitney set up a demonstration for President Thomas Jefferson in 1801. He gave Jefferson and some other government officials piles of musket parts. They randomly chose parts from the piles and gave them to Whitney. He was able to put several muskets together very quickly to prove that his idea worked.

Problem #3: _____

Eli Whitney's Solution: _____

_____

Whitney's idea of interchangeable parts had been used in France several decades before his invention. No one had paid much attention to it. Whitney, however, promoted what he called the "American system." He made interchangeable parts important to mass production. Soon, other gun manufacturers in America and England were using his system. Clock makers began to use interchangeable parts as well.

Name: _____ Date: _____

Learning Textile Terms

Define each of the following words using a dictionary. Then write the word in a sentence.

1. Waterwheel _____

_____

_____

2. Mill _____

_____

_____

3. Textile _____

_____

_____

4. Loom _____

_____

_____

5. Weave _____

_____

_____

6. Spin _____

_____

_____

Name: _____ Date: _____

How Do You Make Clothes?

Read the paragraph and answer the questions.

Even though textile mills began to change the way people made clothes, American women usually made the clothes for everyone in their families until at least 1810. If you have ever made an article of clothing, you know that it is a lot of work! Answer each question below. You may work with a partner.

1. Have you ever sewn a shirt or a pair of pants? _____

2. Do you know anyone who sews all the clothes for his or her family? Who? _____
   _____

3. Even if you do not know much about sewing, think about the steps that you would need to do to make an item of clothing. What would you need to buy? What equipment would you need? Write a paragraph explaining how you would go about making an item of clothing for yourself.

   _____

   _____

   _____

   _____

   _____

4. What would be an advantage of making your own clothes? _____
   _____

5. List two disadvantages of making your own clothes. _____
   _____

6. The list below shows the steps American women once did to make an item of clothing. The list is not in the right order, however. Number the items in sequential order.

   _____ Sew the pieces by hand into pants, shirts, and skirts.

   _____ Obtain cotton fiber.

   _____ Weave the yarn into cloth.

   _____ Spin the clean cotton fiber into yarn.

   _____ Cut the cloth into pieces.

   _____ Make a pattern

Research: Find out how women spun cotton fiber into yarn or how they wove yarn into cloth.

Name: _____ Date: _____

The Effects of Eli Whitney's Cotton Gin

Read the paragraphs below to find out some of the effects of Eli Whitney's invention. Write one effect on each set of lines below.

Eli Whitney learned about the problems of **ginning**, or cleaning, cotton while he was visiting an estate in Georgia. The kind of cotton that grew well in the South was called green seed cotton. The seed of this kind of cotton was almost impossible to separate from the cotton fibers. A slave could only clean one pound of green seed cotton a day.

Plantation owners wanted to find a way to **export**, or send, the cleaned cotton to textile mills in England so that they could make a profit. Inventors had already invented gins to separate the cotton fibers from the seed of the plant. However, those machines were not effective because the seed of the green seed cotton plant clung so tightly to the cotton fibers.

In 1793, Eli Whitney invented a cotton gin that cleaned the cotton much more quickly and much better. As a result, growing cotton soon became profitable. Plantation owners wanted *more* slaves so they could grow even more cotton. Both young and old people who were not strong enough to work at other types of jobs started to work ginning cotton. People paid their debts, and land increased in value. Factories in the North started to use the cotton to make cloth. The shipping industry grew as well.

Effect #1 _____

_____

Effect #2 _____

_____

Effect #3 _____

_____

Effect #4 _____

_____

Effect #5 _____

_____

1. Which effect did you *least* expect from the invention of the cotton gin? Explain your ideas on your own paper.

12

Name: _____ Date: _____

Early American Factories

In 1793, Samuel Slater built the first real American textile mill in Pawtucket, Rhode Island. In a sense, he began the American Industrial Revolution. Slater put several of the processes that were needed to make textiles into one factory. He used a single waterwheel system to power all the machines.

Mr. Slater employed children who were seven to 12 years old to work in his mill. The textile machines were easy to operate, so the children did not need any special skills to run them. In those days, children were already working long hours on their family farms, so no one objected to their working in a mill. Soon other factories started, and more than half of the workers in Rhode Island were children.

The children worked alongside adults in terrible conditions. They started working before sunrise and finished after sunset. An overseer supervised them and often used corporal punishment.

The mills were always dirty and noisy. In winter, the mills were cold and drafty; in summer, they were hot and humid. Many people developed respiratory diseases because of breathing flying lint particles. Although the machines were easy to operate, they were dangerous. If a child was tired or sleepy, he or she could easily lose a finger, an arm, and sometimes, even a scalp!

Back then, only wealthy children had formal schooling. The children who worked in the mills studied basic reading, writing, and arithmetic at Sunday school on their only day off from the mill.

Write your daily schedule in the box below.

Wake-up Time: _____	**Lunch Break:** _____
Leave for School: _____	**Recess Break:** _____
School Starts: _____	**School Ends:** _____
After School Schedule: _____	
_____	

On another sheet of paper, write a paragraph in which you compare and contrast what you do in a day with what a child who worked in Samuel Slater's mill would do in a day. How are your schedules alike? How are they different? What do you do that the children who worked in the mill never had an opportunity to do?

Name: _____ Date: _____

Working at Samuel Slater's Textile Mill

Imagine that you lived in 1796 and had to work in Samuel Slater's textile mill six days a week. In the space below, write three journal entries. In the first entry, describe a typical hot summer day at the mill. In the second entry, describe a typical cold winter day at the mill. Include ideas about what you do at the mill, your working conditions, how the supervisor acts, and how you feel about your work. What do you see, hear, touch, and smell? In the third entry, describe what you do on a Sunday.

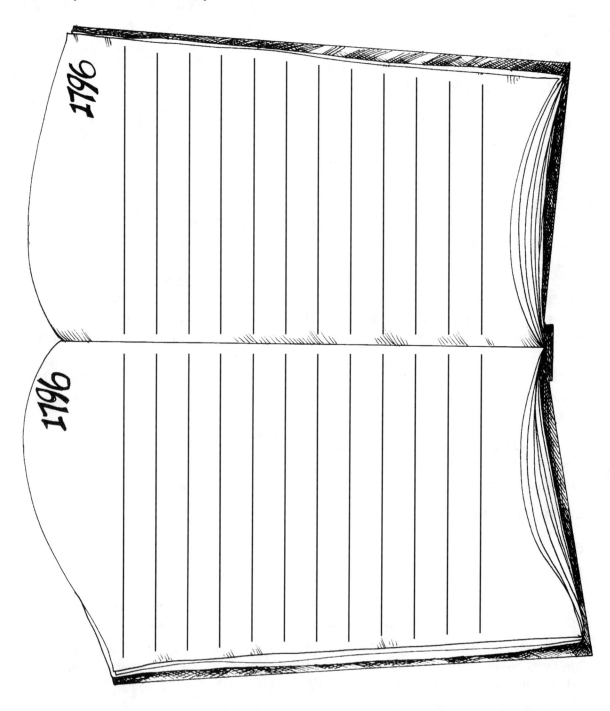

Name: _____ Date: _____

Depending On Credits

Read the paragraph and answer the questions.

Almost all of the 30 employees in Samuel Slater's mill were children. The children lived in housing that he built for them. Then he made them buy everything they needed at his company store. Instead of giving them money for their work, he gave them "credits" to use at his store. He tried to control every part their lives. He controlled how long the children worked and how much money they made. He also built churches and schools near his mill. He made sure that the schools taught what he wanted the children to learn.

Samuel Slater

1. If there were a lot of children available to work in Mr. Slater's mill, do you think he would try to make conditions nicer or worse? Explain your answer.

   _____

   _____

2. If there were only a few children available to work in Mr. Slater's mill, do you think he would try to make conditions nicer or worse? Explain your answer.

   _____

   _____

3. How did giving the workers "credits" instead of money make them dependent on a factory owner?

   _____

   _____

4. More and more workers began to depend on the credits that could only be spent at the company store. What kind of prices might some factory owners charge when everyone had to buy things at their stores? Why do you think that?

   _____

   _____

5. If you had lived back then, would you rather have worked all day long at Samuel Slater's mill or all day long on your family's farm? Why?

   _____

   _____

Name: _____ Date: _____

Meals, Now and Then

Have you ever thought about how easy it is to make breakfast? Answer each question below.

1. You pour a glass of cold milk. Did someone in your family
   _____ buy the milk at a store, or
   _____ milk a cow to get the milk?

2. You scramble some eggs. Did someone in your family
   _____ buy the eggs at a store, or
   _____ gather them from a chicken coop in your backyard?

3. You toast a slice of bread. Did someone in your family
   _____ buy the bread at a store, or
   _____ bake the loaf of bread from scratch?

4. You spread some jam on your toast. Did someone in your family
   _____ buy the jam at a store, or
   _____ make homemade jam?

There's a good chance that your family usually buys the items for meals at a store. Back in 1870, however, most Americans lived on farms or in small agricultural communities. They spent a large part of each day just preparing the food they needed for that day.

Imagine that it is 1870, and that you need to prepare supper for your family. What would you have to do to prepare a supper of chicken, potatoes, pickles, bread, and apple pie? What preparations would you have had to make in advance? Describe your preparations in the box below. Then estimate how long you think these preparations would take.

FOOD/PREPARATION STEPS	PREPARATION TIME
chicken _____	
_____	
_____	_____
potatoes _____	
_____	
_____	_____
pickles _____	
_____	
_____	_____
bread _____	
_____	
_____	_____
apple pie _____	
_____	
_____	

Name: _____ Date: _____

Preserving Food

Read the paragraphs below.

In 1795, Napoleon Bonaparte, the emperor of France, offered a prize for anyone who could come up with a practical method of canning food. He wasn't interested in helping ordinary people find a convenient way to make meals. He just wanted a way to provide good food for his soldiers in battle.

A French chef named Nicolas Appert discovered that he could put soups and stews or small fruits like raspberries and cherries into champagne bottles, seal them, and then plunge the bottles into boiling water. Appert did not understand why this process kept food fresh!

Two industrialists from Britain, John Hall and Bryan Donkin, became interested in Appert's work. They experimented and found that food could be better preserved by using cans made of tinplate sheet iron covered with a thin film of noncorrosive tin. By 1818, they were supplying tens of thousands of cans to the British navy.

At first, canned food was too costly for most people to buy. The food was very popular, however, with soldiers, sailors, and explorers because they could take an adequate supply of food with them wherever they went.

The United States was the first country to mass-produce food in cans. Canned goods then became affordable to most people. Women began to spend less time preparing food. They could create more interesting recipes. The canning industry also helped fishermen and farmers who supplied the food.

As people learned how to preserve food, they experienced many emotions. Choose five words from those listed in the can on the right. Use each word in a sentence that explains why one of the people mentioned in the paragraphs above might have felt that way. An example is given.

WORD BANK

eager	energized
confused	curious
excited	exhausted
relaxed	determined
freed	helpful
ambitious	creative

Example: The women were *energized* because they spent less time preparing meals.

1. _____

   _____

2. _____

3. _____

4. _____

5. _____

Name: _____ Date: _____

Learning Steam Power Terms

Define each of the following words using a dictionary. Draw a picture of *one* of the words in the picture frame below.

1. Steam _____
_____

2. Condenser _____
_____

3. Boiler _____
_____

4. Engine _____
_____

5. Piston _____
_____

6. Rotary motion _____
_____

7. Governor _____
_____

Name: _____ Date: _____

The First True Steam Engine

Read the information below and answer the question.

In the eighteenth century in England, engineers figured out a new way to power machines: steam. Steam power made industrialization grow by leaps and bounds.

1. How does steam power work? Imagine filling a pan with water, covering it with a lid, and putting it on a stove to boil. What will happen to the lid when the water boils?

_____

When water boils, the molecules expand with a tremendous force. As they turn to steam, they can fill a space nearly 2,000 times larger than the volume of the water. That's a lot of power!

Thomas Newcomen, an Englishman, put this power to work by inventing the first true steam engine in 1712. His engine was not very efficient, however. It could only be used for pumping water from coal mines.

Look at the picture of Newcomen's engine. Write the correct word on each line from the list below.

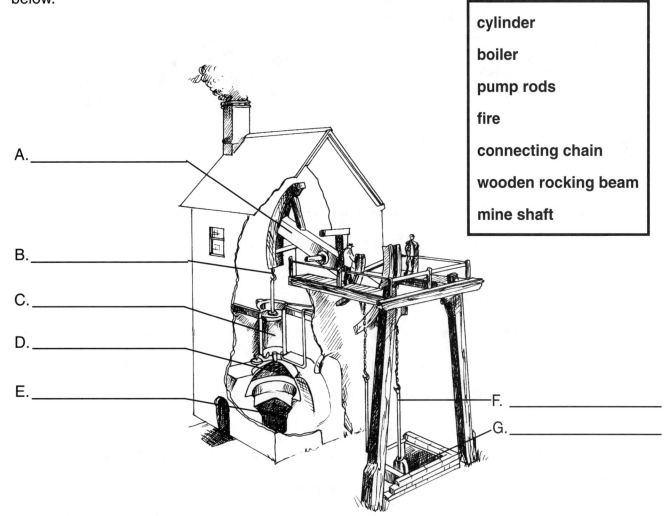

A._____

B._____

C._____

D._____

E._____

F._____

G._____

| cylinder |
| boiler |
| pump rods |
| fire |
| connecting chain |
| wooden rocking beam |
| mine shaft |

Name: _____ Date: _____

James Watt Improves the Steam Engine

James Watt, from Scotland, greatly improved the Newcomen engine 50 years later. Then in 1782, Watt invented a steam engine that could produce **rotary motion**. That invention allowed steam engines to drive rotating shafts, which when connected with canvas belts, could power all kinds of machinery in paper, steel, and textile mills. A rotary engine could also drive the wheels of vehicles.

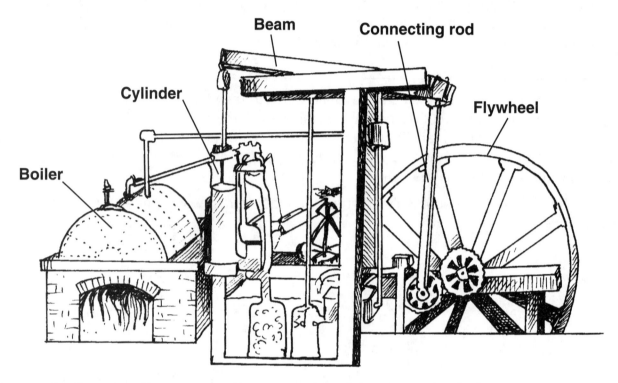

Research: Complete library research on one of the following projects. Share your information with your classmates.

1. List five facts about Thomas Savery or the steam engine he invented.

2. Write a paragraph explaining how Newcomen's steam engine worked.

3. List five facts about Thomas Newcomen.

4. Draw a sketch of Thomas Newcomen's steam engine. Label the parts.

5. Write a paragraph explaining the improvements James Watt made to Newcomen's engine.

6. List five facts about the role Matthew Boulton had in the development of the steam engine.

7. Write a paragraph describing the first steam-driven vehicles.

8. List five fascinating facts about James Watt or his inventions.

9. Write a paragraph about the world's fastest steam car, the *Steamin' Demon*.

10. Find out why Newcomen's engine was inefficient.

Name: _____ Date: _____

Water Power vs. Steam Power

Read each question below. Then answer the question by checking the yes or no column.

	Yes	No
1. Would it be more time-consuming to grind wheat by a water-powered wheel than by hand?		
2. Since water-powered mills were usually built in the countryside, would it be easy to find enough workers?		
3. Would it be difficult to get raw materials to water-powered mills since streams good for power are usually not so good for transportation?		
4. Would it be difficult to get finished goods back to the cities from water-powered mills since streams good for power are usually not so good for transportation?		
5. Might streams and rivers freeze in the wintertime?		
6. Could a steam-powered factory be located in the middle of a city?		
7. Would it be difficult to find workers for a steam-powered factory in a city?		
8. Would a port city with good railroad connections and ship transportation be an ideal location for a steam-powered factory?		
9. Would it be difficult to transport raw materials to a steam-powered factory in a city?		
10. Would it be easy to transport finished goods from a steam-powered factory that was located in a city?		
11. Would New York and Philadelphia likely be among the first cities to become industrialized?		

12. On your own paper, write a paragraph explaining the advantages of steam-powered factories over water-powered factories.

Name: _____ Date: _____

Robert Fulton

Robert Fulton, Jr., was born on a farm in Pennsylvania in 1765. He spent a happy childhood there until he was six years old. His mother particularly loved the farm's flower garden. Unfortunately, his father was not an experienced farmer. After several years of bad weather, the family was forced to sell the farm and move back to Lancaster where his father ran a successful tailoring shop. Two years later, however, Robert Fulton, Sr., became seriously ill and died.

Through his mother's hard work and the help of relatives, Robert was able to attend a private school. Although Fulton wasn't an outstanding student, he had a knack of looking at everyday tasks and finding new and interesting ways to complete them. When candles, which were in short supply, were forbidden at a Fourth of July celebration, he invented a successful skyrocket that he sent blazing upward. He also invented mechanical rowing paddles because he hated rowing the boat when he went fishing with his friends. He conducted many experiments with mercury at the time as well.

Robert Fulton's other interest was painting and drawing. By the time he was 17, he had moved to Philadelphia where he was able to sell some of his oil portraits, watercolor landscapes, and very small paintings called miniatures. He even made enough money to purchase a small farm for his mother in the countryside, complete with space for a flower garden.

1. What two misfortunes happened to the Fulton family when Robert was young?

   _____

   _____

   _____

2. How would the saying "Necessity is the mother of invention" apply to Robert Fulton?

   _____

   _____

   _____

3. From the information in the reading, write two or three words that would describe Robert Fulton. Why did you choose those words?

   _____

   _____

   _____

Name: _____ Date: _____

Robert Fulton (cont.)

Eventually, though, Robert Fulton became quite ill. He went to Europe where he hoped to improve his health and become an even better painter. In Europe, however, there were many struggling painters like himself. Although he could support himself as an artist, he again became more interested in inventing things. It was an exciting time to be in England because the Industrial Revolution was underway. Everywhere he went in Europe, Fulton studied new inventions and met with inventors. Fulton invented a machine to spin flax into linen and a device to twist hemp into rope. He also invented a machine that sawed large slabs of marble into smaller pieces. By 1797, he had even produced a design for a submarine.

Then Fulton met Robert R. Livingston, an American who was living in Europe. Mr. Livingston wanted to find a way to navigate New York's rivers by steamboat. He had the money to finance the project, and Fulton had the engineering ability. Fulton's first attempt at building the steamboat failed, so he had to start over again. By 1803, he had constructed a superior vehicle. He wanted to return to America, but he had to wait two years. The British government would not let anyone take a steam engine out of their country!

Finally, Robert Fulton convinced the British to let him take a single steam engine to America. There he began working on a new steamboat that was 133 feet long and 18 feet wide. This steamboat, which was at first called the *North River Steamboat of Clermont* and later the *Clermont,* traveled about four miles an hour. That was a good speed in those days. The steamboat traveled 150 miles on its first voyage in 1807 from New York City to Albany, the capital of New York state. Although he did not build the first steamboat, Fulton is credited with building the first commercially successful one.

1. List two reasons why Fulton became interested in inventing again.

    _____

    _____

    _____

    _____

2. Why do you think the British government did not want steam engines to leave their country?

    _____

    _____

    _____

    _____

3. On your own paper, write a paragraph from Robert Fulton's point of view. Imagine that you are Fulton, and you are watching your steamboat leave New York City on its first voyage. What are you thinking about? How do you feel? What are you worried about?

Name: _____ Date: _____

Steamships Across America

Research: Complete library research on one of the following projects.

1. Write a paragraph describing the first steamship built by the Marquis Jouffroy d'Abbans. What was the name of the steamboat? Where did it first sail? Why did he abandon any further work on steamships?

2. Write a paragraph describing the steamboat John Fitch invented in 1790. What was the name of the steamboat? Between what two cities did he transport passengers and freight? What did John Fitch prove? What was his main problem with his steamboat?

3. Draw a sketch of John Fitch's steamboat.

4. Write a paragraph describing why Robert Fulton's steamboat was more successful than John Fitch's steamboat. How did the route that the *Clermont* took help Fulton succeed? How did Robert Livingston's involvement help?

5. Write a paragraph describing the steamboat Robert Fulton built in 1811. What was the name of the steamship? What river did it navigate?

6. Write a paragraph describing how steamships promoted settlement and trade.

7. Write a paragraph describing the first steamship to cross the Atlantic in 1819. What was its name? Explain why it was not a true steamship. Why was a rescue ship sent out from Ireland?

Ask classmates to take notes as you read your paragraph or explain your sketch to them. Then ask your classmates three questions about your paragraph or sketch.

Name: _____ Date: _____

Canals

Using the Internet and other reference sources, work with a partner to answer the following questions. Use your own paper if you need more room.

1. What is a canal? _____

_____

2. Why did people build canals? _____

_____

_____

3. What work did the horses and mules do along the canals? _____

_____

_____

4. Were mules or horses faster at pulling a barge? _____

5. Who were the hoggees? What did they do? _____

_____

_____

6. What type of work does a cobbler do? _____

_____

7. Why might the hoggees need a cobbler? _____

_____

_____

8. What could happen to the canals and rivers in the wintertime? _____

_____

9. Why was it easier to haul large loads by canals than by roads? _____

_____

_____

10. What is a lock on a canal?

_____

_____

_____

_____

Name: _____ Date: _____

The Erie Canal

   The most famous canal in America was the Erie Canal. Work began on this canal in 1817. By 1825, it was finished. The canal covered a distance of 363 miles (584 km). It connected New York City with the Great Lakes via the Hudson River.

Look at the map below.

1.   Use an atlas to find the names of the following cities on the map: New York City, Albany, Utica, Syracuse, Rochester, and Buffalo. Write the names in the appropriate places.

2.   Label the Hudson River, the Atlantic Ocean, Lake Erie, and Lake Ontario.

3.   Draw in the route of the Erie Canal.

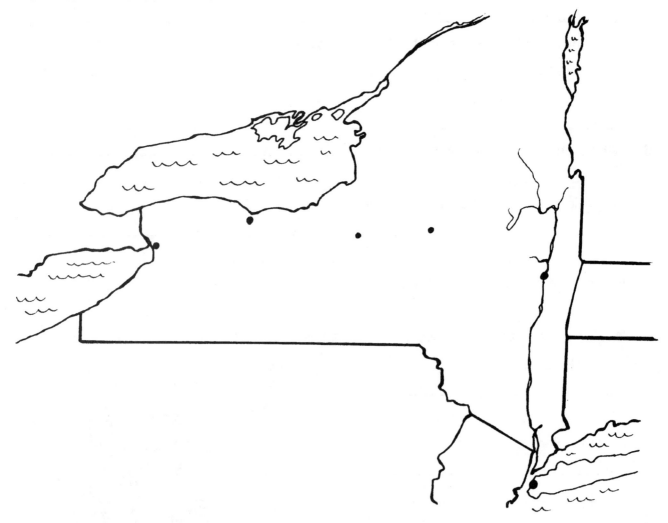

Name: _____   Date: _____

Fascinating Facts About the Erie Canal

Read these fascinating facts about the Erie Canal. Fill in the blanks with words from the box. Use the Internet and other reference sources if you need help.

farmers	Buffalo	cities	Ireland	tolls
one dollar	freight	1817	eastern	mills
85	hostellers	deep	wide	thousands
hoggees	Lake Erie	west	immigration	steam trains

1. Construction on the Erie Canal began in Rome, New York, on July 4, _____.
2. Parts of the canal were built by wealthy _____ along the canal route.
3. Many immigrants from _____ helped build the canal.
4. The laborers received eighty cents to _____ per day for their work.
5. There were _____ locks along the Erie Canal.
6. When the canal was completed in 1825, the governor of New York, De Witt Clinton, sailed from Buffalo to New York City. There, he emptied a barrel of _____ water into the Atlantic Ocean!
7. Farmers started farms throughout the Great Lakes and the Upper Midwest. They shipped their farm products to the _____ part of the United States.
8. The canal helped create many large _____ along its route.
9. _____ were built near the canal. Nearby rivers and streams provided water power. Goods were shipped quickly and cheaply along the canal.
10. The canal encouraged _____ to the Great Lakes area.
11. Consumer goods were shipped _____ along the canal.
12. _____ was shipped along the canal at about 55 miles per 24 hours.
13. People could travel faster than freight along the canal. It only took passengers about four days to travel from New York City to _____.
14. At first, the canal was only four feet (1.2 m) _____. Later, it was deepened to seven feet (2.1 m).
15. At first, the canal was 40 feet (12.2 m) _____. Later it was widened to 70 feet (21.3 m).
16. At first, people had to pay _____ to use the canal.
17. By 1845, _____ of boats used the Erie Canal.
18. A typical crew on a boat included the captain, the steersman, the cook, the deckhand, and the _____. Thousands of people found work as lock tenders, toll collectors, bridge operators, surveyors, repair crews, and bank patrollers.
19. Many merchants, _____ , and shopkeepers lived near the canals to feed, clothe, house, and supply the people who worked on the canals.
20. By the 1850s, people were shipping goods by _____ instead of by canals.

27

Name: _____ Date: _____

Traveling on the Erie Canal

Imagine that you are traveling along the Erie Canal from Buffalo to Albany in 1840. Use the information from the fascinating facts on the previous page to write a journal entry. Describe what you see, hear, taste, touch, and smell along the way.

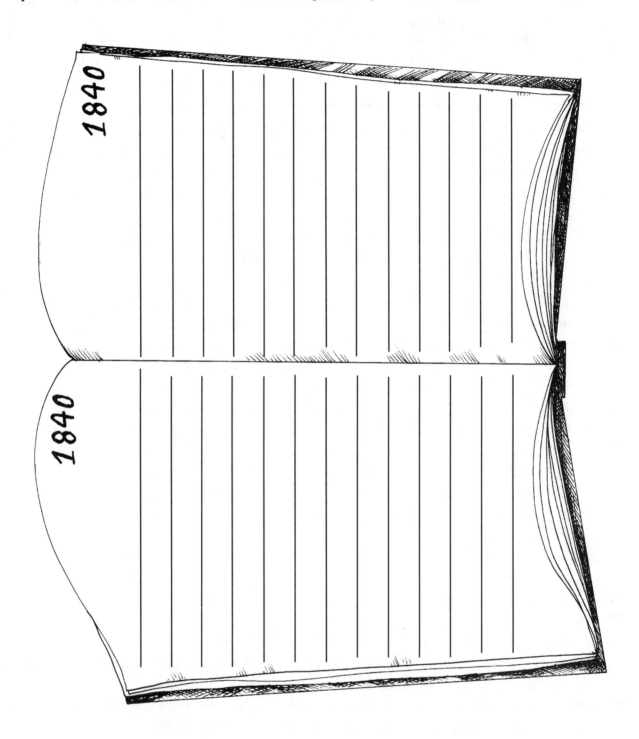

Low Bridge

The Erie Canal even has a well-known song associated with it. It is called the "Erie Canal Song," but it is also known as "Low Bridge." It was published in 1913 to protest the coming of the mechanized barge.

Find the music to this song. Practice singing it with your classmates. If you can play a musical instrument, learn the music and accompany the singers.

The "Erie Canal Song" or "Low Bridge"

1. I've got an old mule and her name is Sal
Fifteen miles on the Erie Canal
She's a good old worker and a good old pal
Fifteen miles on the Erie Canal.

2. We've hauled some barges in our day
Filled with lumber, coal, and hay
And every inch of the way we know
From Albany to Buffalo.

3. Low bridge, everybody down
Low bridge for we're coming to a town
And you'll always know your neighbor
And you'll always know your pal
If you've ever navigated on
The Erie Canal.

4. We'd better get along on our way, old gal
Fifteen miles on the Erie Canal
'Cause you bet your life I'd never part with Sal
Fifteen miles on the Erie Canal.

5. Git up there mule, here comes a lock
We'll make Rome 'bout six o'clock
One more trip and back we'll go
Right back home to Buffalo.

6. Low bridge, everybody down
Low bridge for we're coming to a town
And you'll always know your neighbor
And you'll always know your pal
If you've ever navigated on
The Erie Canal.

Name: _____ Date: _____

All About Iron

Answer the following questions. Work with a partner to answer the following questions. Use the Internet and other reference sources if you need help.

1. What do you think people made tools out of before they had iron?

   _____

   _____

2. What would be the problem with these kinds of materials?

   _____

   _____

3. During the Iron Age, which was about 3,500 years ago, the Hittites learned how to make tools out of iron. What advantage would iron tools have?

   _____

   _____

4. Iron was an ideal metal because it could be melted, shaped, hammered, and cast. However, it was very difficult to get the iron out of the iron ore. What is iron ore?

   _____

5. The blast furnace was first invented during the Middle Ages. A blast furnace was a huge, stone oven in which charcoal, iron ore, and limestone was burned. The charcoal became very hot and made carbon monoxide. It reacted chemically with the iron ore to separate out the impurities from the metal. What pure metal was left?

   _____

6. In the late 1700s, Abraham Darby III built the first iron bridge across the River Severn in England. It is still there today. He showed that iron was an ideal material for building large structures. What else besides bridges would benefit from an iron framework?

   _____

   _____

7. Why would an iron-framed building be ideal for a textile mill?

   _____

   _____

   _____

Name: _____ Date: _____

Taller and Taller Buildings

Read the paragraphs and work with a partner to answer the following questions. Use the Internet and other reference sources if you need help.

1. Cast iron began to be used for buildings as well as bridges. In 1851, the Great Exhibition was held in London. The exhibit hall had 300,000 panes of glass in a huge iron frame that covered 2,000 acres and held eight miles of display tables. The exhibition showed how far-reaching industrialism had become in Britain.

   What was the name of the exhibit hall? _____

2. For the Paris Exhibition of 1889, a famous iron building was constructed.

   What is the name of this tower that is still standing in Paris? _____

3. After a while, cast iron was replaced by rolled steel. Architects in the United States started to use steel frames. The first skyscraper in America was built in 1885 in Chicago.

   What was the name of this ten-story-high building? _____

4. Architects next began to use reinforced concrete, which is liquid concrete poured over steel rods. The first large skyscraper made of steel and concrete was the Woolworth Building in New York City in 1913. It was 794 feet high (242 meters).

   How many stories did this building have? _____

5. Architects continued to build skyscrapers in America because of the shortage of land in cities. In 1931, the Empire State Building was opened in New York.

   How tall was this building? _____

6. In 1974, the Sears Tower opened in Chicago.

   How tall was this building? _____

7. How tall is the CN Tower in Toronto, Canada? _____

8. Do you think taller buildings are better than shorter buildings? Explain your ideas.

   _____

   _____

   _____

   _____

Research: Is there a limit to how tall a skyscraper can be built? What is your reasoning?

Name: _____ Date: _____

Inventing a Safe Elevator

Read the story about the invention of the elevator. Fill in the blanks with words from the box.

mass-produced	**possible**	**stairs**	**hoists**
standard-sized	**World's Fair**	**elevator**	**cut**
safety mechanism	**New York City**	**cables**	**Otis**

In 1847, James Bogardus built a five-story factory in (1) _____ made out of cast-iron. He also built other factories using (2) _____ parts. These were the first (3) _____ buildings.

As buildings got higher, goods were brought up from floor to floor by mechanical (4) _____. Sometimes the (5) _____ on these hoists broke, so people did not want to use them. Understandably, they also did not want to climb up flight after flight of 6) _____.

This problem was solved by Elisha (7) _____, who was an engineer from Vermont. He invented a (8) _____ to hold the hoist in place even if the cables slipped or broke. He used a series of vertical pieces to grab the (9) _____ in case of an accident. Otis showed the public at the (10) _____ in 1853 that his invention was safe. He got into an elevator, which was then lifted high up into the air. The cables were then (11) _____, but the elevator did not crash.

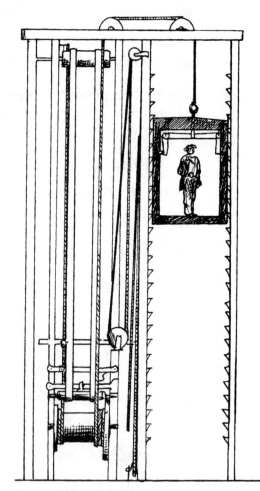

By 1857, the first safety elevator was installed in a New York City department store. Today's skyscrapers would not be (12) _____ if the elevator had not been invented.

Name: _____   Date: _____

Riding the Rails

Imagine that you are a news reporter covering the events below. You only have time to ask *one* question at each event. Write down the question you would ask. It should be the kind of question whose answer would help you write an interesting news article about the event. The first one is done for you.

1. It is February 13, 1804. In southern Wales, Richard Trevithick is demonstrating the first steam locomotive, called the *New Castle*. The engine is pulling a loaded coal train for nine miles along a track. Before this time, horses have always pulled trains.

    Example Question: Do you think a steam engine could ever transport people?

2. It is 1821. George Stephenson's steam locomotive, called the *Locomotion,* is giving 400 excited passengers a ride from Stockton to Darlington in England.

    Your question: _____

3. It is 1829. George Stephenson and his son Robert are entering a more powerful locomotive, called the *Rocket,* into a competition with two other trains to see whose will be the fastest. They will also be competing against two horse teams.

    Your question: _____

4. It is 1830. A steam locomotive called the *John Bull* has arrived in America. It was built by the same company that made Stephenson's *Rocket.*

    Your question: _____

5. It is 1869. The tracks of the Central Pacific and the Union Pacific railways are being linked together at Promontory Point, Utah. This will be the first transcontinental railroad.

    Your question: _____

6. It is 1964. You are in Tokyo, Japan, awaiting the arrival of the first "Bullet" train from Osaka. The train is traveling at 130 miles per hour (210 km/h).

    Your question: _____

7. It is 1990. You are in France. A French train, called the *TGV,* reaches a speed of 320 miles per hour (515 km/h). It runs on high-speed tracks.

    Your question: _____

Name: _____   Date: _____

How Did Steam Locomotives Affect America?

Many changes took place as railroads were built and steam locomotives began to cross America. Read each statement below. If you think the statement tells about a change that was at least partly due to the railroads or steam locomotives, put a plus sign (+) on the line. If you think the statement tells about a change that was not due to the railroads or steam locomotives, put a minus sign (-) on the line. The first one is done for you.

__+__   1. People began to ship fewer goods by canals.

_____   2. It was easier to transport goods and people to the interior part of America.

_____   3. More iron and steel were produced.

_____   4. More coal was produced.

_____   5. Big cities and little towns were connected via the railroads.

_____   6. It was easier to transport coal to factories.

_____   7. Business became nationwide.

_____   8. More Americans and European immigrants settled land in the interior part of America.

_____   9. Farmers could transport agricultural products to new markets.

_____   10. New towns were set up along the railroads.

_____   11. Ranchers could transport their cattle to markets.

_____   12. More telegraph lines were set up.

_____   13. Many people found jobs laying track.

_____   14. Air pollution increased.

_____   15. More raw materials and finished goods were transported from one region to another.

_____   16. The western part of the country was linked to the eastern part of the country.

Choose one of the statements above. In a short paragraph, explain how the railroads and steam locomotives helped to bring about that change.

Name: _____ Date: _____

Samuel Morse

Read the story about Samuel Morse on this page and the next two pages. As you read, answer the questions about the ingredients that helped Samuel become an inventor.

You may already know that Samuel Morse invented the telegraph. You probably also realize that the idea for a telegraph just didn't "spring out" of his head one day. He had to study in school and get some experience inventing things. His knowledge and experience were two of the "ingredients" that helped him become an inventor.

Samuel Morse was born in 1791. He disliked school except for his interest in electricity and art. Although his parents could barely afford it, they sent Samuel to London to study art. In time, he became an excellent painter. He returned to America hoping to paint portraits of Americans for a living. It was difficult to find customers, so he had to travel from town to town. In 1818, he married Lucretia Pickering, and they eventually had three children.

1.   The first ingredient was *interest.* What interested Samuel most at school?

    _____

Samuel had a difficult time supporting his family as an artist. He tried to make money by doing other things, such as inventing a water pump for firefighters and a marble-cutting machine. Although neither idea was a success, he gained experience inventing things.

2.   The second ingredient was *experience.* In what did Samuel gain experience?

    _____

Samuel's wife died in 1825 of heart trouble. Sadly, Samuel placed his children with family members, and then he returned to Europe for more training as an artist. His dream was to be chosen as one of the artists who would paint a mural in the rotunda of the U. S. Capitol. While he was in France, he learned about the semaphore telegraph system. In this system, tall platforms, or **semaphores**, were placed about 15 miles apart from each other. A man stood at the top of each semaphore and held up a huge code for the next person to see. Then the message was repeated to the next semaphore. Of course, this system didn't work on foggy days. Morse's knowledge about the semaphore system helped him think about how messages could be sent over long distances.

3.   The third ingredient was *knowledge.* Samuel became knowledgeable about

    _____

    _____

Name: _____ Date: _____

Samuel Morse (cont.)

On the ship home from Europe, Samuel heard the passengers talking about electricity. He already had an interest in electricity, experience as an inventor, and knowledge about the semaphore system. Now he had an inspiration—a new idea—that electricity might be able to transmit messages. He developed a simple electric telegraph system on the trip home.

4. The fourth ingredient was *inspiration*. Samuel's inspiration was that _____

_____

Samuel Morse was practical. He didn't need fancy materials for his invention. He used an ordinary picture frame, a table, and piece of lead that he melted and molded. His system was simple, and it worked!

5. The fifth ingredient was *practicality*. Samuel was practical because _____

_____

Everyone ignored Samuel's invention. He needed money, so he became a professor of painting and sculpture at the University of the City of New York. When he learned that his dream to paint a mural in the rotunda had fallen through, he never painted seriously again. He started to work on the telegraph once more. He had to make his own supplies, including buying wire in pieces, joining it together, and insulating it with cotton. In 1837, he strung ten miles of wire around his classroom, then invited wealthy businessmen in for a demonstration. After that, Samuel formed a partnership with two other men, and together they continued to improve the telegraph.

6. The sixth ingredient was *perseverance*. Perseverance means "not quitting." In what way was Samuel perseverant?

_____

_____

_____

Samuel asked the U.S. Congress for money to test the telegraph, but Congress was not interested. No one in France and England was interested either. Finally in 1842, he hand-wrapped two miles of wire in cotton, tar, and rubber. He hired a man to row him across New York harbor so he could lay the cable. He stationed a telegraph operator on each side of the harbor. Everything worked and was set to go. Then, fishermen pulled up the cable and cut it because they didn't know what it was! The demonstration had to be canceled. People thought Samuel was a liar and a fraud. But Samuel had his convictions. He believed that his invention would be important someday.

Name: _____   Date: _____

Samuel Morse (cont.)

7. The seventh ingredient was *conviction.* Samuel believed that _____

_____

_____

  A few months later, Samuel asked Congress again for money to test the telegraph. It wasn't until 1844 that Congress passed his request by just a few votes at the very last moment. During the next two months, Samuel and his partners laid a telegraph line between Baltimore, Maryland, and Washington, D.C. Once again, things did not proceed easily. They buried the cable beside the railroad track, then discovered that the wire was not properly insulated. Fortunately, Samuel was a creative person and was able to figure out a new way to remedy the problem. Without much time left, he decided to string the wire from tall poles above the ground.

8. The eighth ingredient was *creativity.* Samuel showed his creativity by

_____

_____

  On May 24, 1844, Samuel Morse sat in the Supreme Court building in Washington, D.C. and tapped out the message, "What hath God wrought!" The message was received forty miles away in Baltimore. After that, the telegraph was a success. By 1852, there were telegraph lines all across North America and Europe. By 1866, a telegraph cable even crossed the Atlantic Ocean!

  Even if you are not planning to become an inventor, the "ingredients" that helped Samuel Morse become an inventor can help you become a more creative and interesting person. On your own paper, write a paragraph about how one of the ingredients could help you achieve your goals in the future.

Name: _____ Date: _____

Morse Code

A telegraph works by allowing signals to be sent along a wire. At first, telegraphs were used by the railroads to keep track of trains. Later, telegraph cables linked major cities. Today, Morse code, the system of signals devised by Morse, has been largely replaced by modern communication systems. Morse code is mainly used by amateur radio operators all around the world.

Morse code uses a system of signals to send messages. The signals are made up of short dots (short electric pulses) and long dashes (longer electric pulses) that represent the letters of the alphabet and the numerals 0 through 9.

Study the code below, and then figure out each of the messages.

A	• –	H	• • • •	O	– – –	U	• • –
B	– • • •	I	• •	P	• – – •	V	• • • –
C	– • – •	J	• – – –	Q	– – • –	W	• – –
D	– • •	K	– • –	R	• – •	X	– • • –
E	•	L	• – • •	S	• • •	Y	– • – –
F	• • – •	M	– –	T	–	Z	– – • •
G	– – •	N	– •				

1. What does the message say?

    • • •   – – –   • • •

    ____   ____   ____

2. What does the message say?

    – – •   – – –   – – –   – • •   – • • •   – • – –   •

    ____   ____   ____   ____   ____   ____   ____

Research: With an adult's help, you can learn how to make a simple telegraph set. The book, *Samuel Morse* by Mona Kerby and published by Franklin Watts, gives complete instructions. Even if you don't have a telegraph, you could tap out the code with your finger or a pencil.

On your own sheet of paper, write a message for a friend using Morse code. Use three spaces between letters and six spaces between words.

Name: _____ Date: _____

Alike and Different

How were Samuel Morse and Robert Fulton alike? How were they different from each other? Look at the words and phrases below. Which ones apply only to Samuel Morse? Which ones apply only to Robert Fulton? Which words or phrases apply to both men? Fill in the boxes below to show how these men were alike and how they were different from one another. You may refer back to the pages on Morse and Fulton for help.

Robert Fulton

Samuel Morse

Perseverant

Experienced hardships

Born in 1765

Invented several things

Wanted to be a painter

Born in 1791

Studied art in Europe

Early interest in electricity

Early interest in finding new ways to complete tasks

SAMUEL MORSE	BOTH MEN	ROBERT FULTON

Name: _____ Date: _____

Disappointment and Perseverance

So many of the inventors that you have read about experienced disappointments in their lives. For example, Samuel Morse was an excellent painter, but he had a difficult time supporting his family as an artist. He tried to paint portraits for a living, but it was difficult to find customers. He had to travel from town to town looking for work. He also studied art in Europe in the hopes that he would be selected as one of the painters for a mural in the rotunda of the U.S. Capitol. It was a huge disappointment for him when he was not selected.

1. Why do you think inventors like Morse succeeded in spite of the disappointments in their lives?

   _____

   _____

   _____

2. Most everyone experiences some disappointment in his or her life. What disappointment have you or someone you know experienced?

   _____

   _____

   _____

   _____

3. Did that disappointment help you or someone you know in some way?

   _____

   _____

   _____

4. Many of the inventors that you read about were perseverant. They didn't give up in spite of the fact that they had failures along the way. Robert Fulton's first steamboat, for example, sank and splintered into pieces. In the long run, however, the inventors' perseverance paid off. In what ways have you or someone you know been perseverant? How did your perseverance pay off in the long run?

   _____

   _____

   _____

   _____

Name: _____ Date: _____

Learning Electricity Terms

Match each word to its definition. Use the Internet and other reference sources if you need help.

_____ 1. A piece of equipment that changes the voltage of an electric current.

_____ 2. This word is the shortened form of dynamoelectric. It is another name for a generator.

_____ 3. A place that houses the dynamo or generator.

_____ 4. An engine that is driven by water, steam, or gas passing through the blades of a wheel and making it revolve.

_____ 5. A form of energy caused by the motion of electrons and protons. It can be produced by rotating a magnet within a coil of wire.

_____ 6. A machine that provides the power to make something run or work.

_____ 7. A machine that produces electricity by turning a magnet inside a coil of wire.

_____ 8. The movement of electricity through a wire.

A. Electricity

B. Motor

C. Turbine

D. Electric current

E. Transformer

F. Dynamo

G. Power station

H. Generator

Name: _____ Date: _____

A History of Electricity

Read each paragraph. Find the sentence in each paragraph that does not belong there. Cross it out.

1. Throughout most of history, people did not know much about electricity. At first, people only knew about electricity in the form of lightning. Lightning frightened many people. The ancient Greeks discovered that rubbing amber, a fossilized gum from trees, made it attract objects such as feathers or straw. That was what we now call static electricity.

2. In the 1600s, scientists in Europe began to experiment with electricity. They realized that a machine in which a piece of cloth was rubbed continuously against a glass plate would produce a flow or current of electricity. Then Pieter van Musschenbroek, a professor of physics at Leyden University in the Netherlands, realized that an electric current could be stored for a brief time in a jar of water. The Netherlands is a small country in Europe. The spark from it could give an electric shock. His device was called the Leyden jar.

3. In America, Benjamin Franklin first proved that lightning was a form of electricity. During a thunderstorm in 1752, he flew a kite that had a key tied to the end of the string. When lightning hit the kite, a current of static electricity flowed down the string into the key and then onto the ground. That caused a series of sparks. When Franklin connected the kite to a Leyden jar, the water in the jar became electrically charged. Those sparks were amazing. Franklin figured out that the sparks were caused by negative and positive charges being brought together.

4. In 1800, an Italian professor, Alessandro Volta, invented several devices for storing electricity. Electricity was an interesting subject. Then in 1820, a Danish scientist named Hans Christian Oersted discovered the link between magnetism and electricity. When Oersted placed a compass near a wire carrying an electric current, the needle in the compass moved. He realized that electrical energy could be converted into mechanical energy. Electricity could make things move!

5. In 1821, an English scientist, Michael Faraday, showed that electricity could produce rotary motion. He also made the first electric dynamo in 1831. Practical generators were not available, though, until the 1870s. I wonder why it took so long.

6. In 1879, Thomas Edison invented the electric light bulb. Edison also invented the phonograph. Because the light bulbs were safe to use in homes, everyone wanted to have electric power. Edison figured out how to mass-produce lights. He developed supply systems and built the first power station in 1881. Electric power began to replace steam power.

Name: _____ Date: _____

How Does Electricity Affect the Earth?

space	temperature	steam	heat	fossil
decreasing	greenhouse	increasing	magic	oxygen
generators	coal	reduce	renewable	energy
water	turbines	nuclear	iron	waves
carbon dioxide				

Fill in the sentences using the words in the box above. You will not need all the words.

1. Electricity requires energy, which is produced by ___ ___ ___ ⃝ .

2. The coal heats the water and turns it into ___⃝___ ___ ___ .

3. The steam powers the turbines, which drive the electric ___ ___ ___ ___ ___ ⃝ ___ ___ .

4. Burning coal produces a gas called ___ ___ ___ ___ ___ ___ ___⃝___ ___ ___ .

5. The amount of carbon dioxide in the air is ___ ___ ⃝___ ___ ___ ___ ___ .

6. The sun's heat reaches the earth. The carbon dioxide traps the ___⃝___ ___ that is radiated back from the earth's surface.

7. The heat does not escape into space. This is called the ___ ___⃝___ ___ ___ ___ ___ ___ effect. This may cause the earth's temperature to rise quickly.

8. Many nations are trying to ___ ___ ___ ___⃝___ the amount of carbon dioxide that they produce.

9. Coal, gas, and oil are called ___ ___ ___ ___⃝___ fuels. They will eventually be used up.

10. Some ___ ___ ___ ___ ___⃝ sources do not get used up. They are called renewable sources of energy.

11. ___ ___⃝___ ___ ___ ___ energy might work if the risks of accidents could be lessened.

12. Write the letters in circles here: ___ ___ ___ ___ ___ ___ ___ ___ ___ ___

13. Unscramble the circled letters and write the word on the line. _____

Name: _____ Date: _____

List Fifteen

1. Box #1: List fifteen items in your home that run on electricity.

2. Box #2: List fifteen things you would have to do differently if you did not have electricity.

Box #1	Box #2
1. _____	1. _____
2. _____	2. _____
3. _____	3. _____
4. _____	4. _____
5. _____	5. _____
6. _____	6. _____
7. _____	7. _____
8. _____	8. _____
9. _____	9. _____
10. _____	10. _____
11. _____	11. _____
12. _____	12. _____
13. _____	13. _____
14. _____	14. _____
15. _____	15. _____

Name: _____ Date: _____

Thomas Edison Crossword Puzzle

Use the clues below to complete the crossword puzzle.

Across

2. During his lifetime, Edison registered 1,093 _____.
5. Edison's favorite invention was the _____.
8. When Thomas Edison was ten years old, he set up his own _____ at home.
9. When Edison was asked about his _____, he said, "I'll retire the day before my funeral."

Down

1. Edison built the world's first power station in 1881. The Pearl Street Station relied on steam from burning coal to power the _____.
2. Thomas Edison said, "Genius is one percent inspiration and ninety-nine percent _____."
3. People were so amazed by the phonograph that Edison was called "The _____ of Menlo Park."
4. Thomas Edison was the most _____ inventor of his day.
6. The first recording was the nursery _____, "Mary Had a Little Lamb."
7. In 1879, Edison created the electric _____ lamp, which burned for 45 hours.

Name: _____ Date: _____

Hello, How Are You?

Read the paragraphs about how a telephone works. Then number the statements below in the correct sequence.

How do you call a friend on the telephone? You just pick up the phone and key in the number. But what *really* happens when you speak into the mouthpiece? The sound of your voice makes a flat piece of metal in the mouthpiece vibrate. That stretches and squashes tiny carbon granules that are stored in a container of the mouthpiece. Electricity travels through those carbon granules, allowing the sound of your voice to be converted into fast-changing electrical pulses or signals.

What *really* happens when your friend answers the telephone and says "Hello?" Your friend can hear your voice because the signals have traveled along the wires to the earpiece of his or her telephone. The signals pass through a coil of wire that is called an electromagnet. That produces magnetism that pulls on a sheet of metal in the earpiece. The strength of the magnetism varies with the fast-changing signals, making the metal move back and forth very quickly. These are the sound waves that your friend hears.

A. _____ A flat piece of metal in the mouthpiece vibrates.

B. _____ The metal in the earpiece moves back and forth quickly.

C. _____ Your friend answers the telephone.

D. _____ The signals pass through an electromagnet.

E. _____ The signals travel along the wires to the earpiece of your friend's telephone.

F. _____ The magnetism pulls on a sheet of metal in the earpiece.

G. _____ Your voice is converted into fast-changing electrical sounds and pulses.

H. _____ Electricity travels through the carbon granules.

I. _____ You call a friend.

J. _____ Tiny carbon granules are stretched and squashed in a container of the mouthpiece.

K. _____ The strength of the magnetism varies with the fast-changing signals.

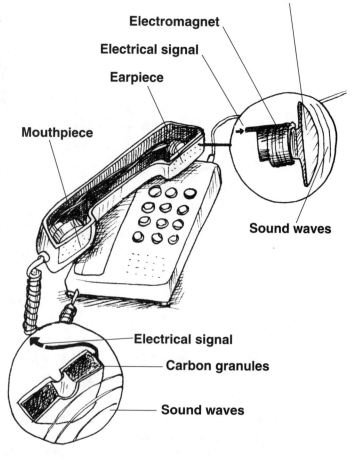

Thin metal sheet
Electromagnet
Electrical signal
Earpiece
Mouthpiece
Sound waves
Electrical signal
Carbon granules
Sound waves

Name: _____ Date: _____

One Thing Affects Another

During industrialization, a change in one area often brought about changes in other areas. Read each section below and fill in the cause or the effect.

1. Steam-powered factories needed a lot of coal to heat the boilers. As a result, the coal industry boomed.

   Cause: Steam-powered factories needed a lot of coal to heat the boilers.

   Effect: _____

2. The coal industry, however, needed trains with powerful engines and strong rails made of high quality steel to bring the coal to the factories. Fortunately, at that same time, a technology that allowed the production of large quantities of high-quality steel came along. Therefore, many railroads were built in the United States.

   Cause: _____

   _____

   Effect: Many railroads were built in the United States.

3. Because of all the new railroads, the mail delivery was speeded up.

   Cause: _____

   Effect: _____

4. The invention of the telegraph by Samuel Morse speeded up communication even more. Americans could quickly find out prices from distant cities and place orders. The quick exchange of information also allowed newspapers to report news from across the nation. Even railroad engineers used the telegraph to find out exactly where the trains were at any moment.

   Cause: The telegraph speeded up communication even more.

   Effect #1: _____

   Effect #2: _____

   Effect #3: _____

Name: _____ Date: _____

One Thing Affects Another (cont.)

Read each section below and fill in the cause or the effect.

5. In the 1860s, a British scientist named James Maxwell showed that invisible waves should be given off by a high-frequency oscillating electric current. A high-frequency oscillating current is one that changes directions thousands of times each second. In 1888, German scientist Heinrich Hertz used that information to build an electrical gadget that gave off invisible waves. These "radio" waves could be detected by another gadget nine feet away. That was the first radio transmission.

    Cause: James Maxwell showed that invisible waves should be given off by an oscillating electric current.

    Effect: _____

    _____

6. Guglielmo Marconi, an Italian scientist, varied the waves so that they could carry messages. Unlike a telephone, however, there was no wire between the sender and the receiver. He invented what became known as the "wireless." In 1901, he was able to send radio messages all the way from Europe to North America.

    Cause: _____

    _____

    Effect: He could send radio messages all the way from Europe to North America.

7. At first, the radio messages used Morse code dots and dashes. Later, radio receivers were able to change the waves into electrical signals and feed them into a loudspeaker to make sounds. In the 1920s, home radios became common.

    Cause: Radio receivers were able to convert radio waves into electrical signals.

    Effect: _____

8. Scientists found ways to send pictures by radio waves. In the 1920s, Vladimir Zworking devised the electronic television system we use today.

    Cause: _____

    Effect: _____

    _____

Name: _____ Date: _____

Get the Message?

Read the information and answer the questions. Use your own paper if you need more room.

1. A long time ago, North American Plains Indians used smoke signals to send messages. What types of messages do you think might have been sent by smoke signals?

   _____

2. By 1830, people knew about batteries. They realized that if they just had very long wires, they could send electric signals over long distances. Then Samuel Morse invented the telegraph, and in 1844, he sent the first long-distance message. What were his words?

   _____

3. By 1852, there were telegraph lines all across North America and Europe. By 1866, a telegraph cable crossed the Atlantic Ocean! If you had been the first to send a message across the ocean, what would it have said?

   _____

4. Next, inventors wanted to figure out how to change the pattern of someone's voice into electrical signals. Alexander Graham Bell did just that in 1876 when he invented a simple machine that changed sound to electrical signals. The first words that he spoke on the telephone were an accident. He had just spilled some acid in his workroom, so he called for help on his test system to his assistant Thomas Watson who was in the next room. If you had invented the telephone and wanted your words to be memorable, what would you have said?

   _____

   _____

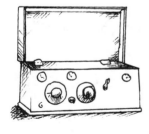

5. In 1901, Guglielmo Marconi sent radio messsages across the Atlantic Ocean from England to North America. What message would you have sent?

   _____

   _____

6. In 1969, Neil Armstrong sent a message from the moon to the earth. What did his message say?

   _____

Name: _____ Date: _____

Into the Air!

If you have ever taken an airplane flight, you know that it can be a relaxing experience. You sit in a comfortable seat watching television or listening to music. An attendant serves you a snack or a meal. In a few hours, you can travel thousands of miles.

It wasn't like that on the first flight back in 1903. On that flight, Orville Wright had to lie on his stomach between the wings of a machine that looked like an oversized kite. The flight lasted just 12 seconds and covered only 120 feet. After the *Flyer* landed, a gust of wind caught it and wrecked it! Still, Orville Wright was the first person to make a powered flight in a heavier-than-air machine. Orville and his brother Wilbur didn't give up, though. By 1906, they had built an airplane that could stay in the air for 38 minutes and cover nearly 25 miles.

Many European governments became interested in flying. In 1914, at the start of World War I, pilots first used aircraft to check enemy positions. Later, planes were used for aerial combat and to bomb troops and civilians. After the war, pilots set up the first airmail and passenger services.

Many metal-framed bombers were built and used in World War II. After the war ended in 1945, airlines set up passenger services crisscrossing the world. Airplanes were also used to take injured people to hospitals; to deliver urgently needed medicine, food, and supplies; and to help farmers with their crops.

Although Wilbur Wright died suddenly in 1912, Orville Wright lived until 1948. Think of all the changes in aviation he experienced during his lifetime!

Research: Complete library research on one of the following projects:

1. Imagine that you are Orville Wright. The year is 1903. In a poem or in a paragraph, tell what it was like to be the first person to fly in a machine-powered airplane.

2. Write several paragraphs or a poem describing Charles Lindbergh's solo flight across the Atlantic Ocean in 1927.

3. Draw a picture of Charles Lindbergh's plane, *The Spirit of St. Louis.*

4. Write several paragraphs or a poem describing Amelia Earhart's 1932 solo flight across the Atlantic Ocean.

5. Imagine that you are Orville Wright in 1945, reflecting about the history of the airplane. Describe the good things and the bad things that happened as a result of your invention.

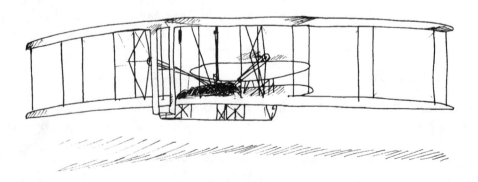

Name: _____ Date: _____

Making Cars on an Assembly Line

1. What is the dullest job you could imagine doing when you're an adult?

   _____

2. Explain why that job would be so dull.

   _____

   _____

Workers at the Ford Plant in Detroit in 1908 also knew the meaning of the word *dull*. As a bare car chassis moved quickly along a conveyor belt, a worker put the same part or parts on each car. By the time the car rolled off the assembly line, the car was complete. The work required no skill or craftsmanship by the worker. The work was so dull that many workers just quit. Ford stopped some of the people from quitting by offering them five dollars a day. Back then, most people made about fourteen dollars a week, so five dollars a day was a very good wage.

3. Would you be willing to work at a very dull job all your life if you received good wages? Why or why not?

   _____

   _____

4. By using an assembly line, Ford was able to build 730,000 cars a year. Before he introduced the assembly line, he was only able to build 11,000 cars a year. What other kinds of products beside cars could be more easily produced by using an assembly line?

   _____

5. Ford did not want to make luxury cars for rich people. Instead, he wanted to make cars that were affordable to the thousands of isolated farmers who lived in the interior of America. Why was that a good marketing plan?

   _____

   _____

6. The Model T was introduced in 1908. It was a popular car because it was easy to maintain and repair. It also rode high above the ground. What advantage would that give it?

   _____

   _____

7. Take a survey in your classroom. How many students' families own Ford cars or trucks?

   _____

Name: _____ Date: _____

Before 1870 and After 1900

What a difference 30 years can make! Between 1870 and 1900, life in America changed significantly. Look at the statements listed below. Decide which statements were more typical for Americans *before* 1870 and which statements were more typical for Americans *after* 1900. Write "1870" or "1900" on the blank before each statement.

_____ 1. Most Americans lived on farms or in small farm communities.

_____ 2. Almost half of Americans lived in cities.

_____ 3. Many Americans were working in mills and factories.

_____ 4. Most Americans got their milk directly from cows.

_____ 5. Most American women washed clothes in buckets.

_____ 6. Most Americans bought ready-made goods in stores.

_____ 7. Most Americans had to draw their bathwater in buckets from wells and then heat the water on the stove.

_____ 8. Bread and jelly were sold in local retail stores.

_____ 9. Fields were plowed with oxen and mules.

_____ 10. Women ironed clothes with flatirons that had been heated on stoves.

In the picture frame on the left, draw a picture of some aspect of American life before 1870. In the picture frame on the right, draw a picture of the same aspect of American life after 1900.

Before 1870	**After 1900**

Name: _____ Date: _____

Industrial Mathematics

1. In 1870, almost three-fourths of Americans lived on farms or in small farming communities. What fraction of Americans lived in *cities?* _____

2. By 1900, almost one-half of Americans lived in cities. What fraction of Americans lived on farms or in small farming communities? _____

3. In 1875, about 157,000 tons of steel were produced in the United States. By 1910, it was 26 million tons. How many years did it take for this increase in production? _____

4. By 1910, there were 90 buildings in New York and Chicago with more than 10 stories. By 1920, the number had grown to 450. How many more buildings with more than 10 stories were there in 1920 than in 1910? _____

5. In 1870, there were 2,600 telephones in the United States. Three years later, there were an additional 45,400 telephones in the United States. How many telephones were there in 1873? _____

6. The Erie Canal was 360 miles long. How many kilometers is that? _____

7. A blast furnace today can make about 5,000 tons of iron every day. How many tons of iron can a blast furnace make in seven days? _____

8. In 1882, factories in the United States made 100,000 light bulbs. By 1900, factories made 35 million. How many years did it take to see this increase in production? _____

9. The price of a car dropped from $850 to $360. How much less did someone pay for a car after the price dropped?

_____

10. Before Ford built his assembly line, his company could build 11,000 cars per year. After he introduced the assembly line, his company could make 730,000 cars per year. How many more cars could he make per year with the assembly line than without it?

_____

Name: _____ Date: _____

Power Statements

Read each statement below. Write "T" for true or "F" for false on the line in front of each statement.

_____ 1. Waterwheels and windmills could be used to grind grain.

_____ 2. Waterwheels and windmills always worked.

_____ 3. Steam engines were the first reliable source of power.

_____ 4. Steam-powered factories could be located only in the countryside.

_____ 5. Many people moved to cities where steam-powered factories were located.

_____ 6. Steam-powered factories did not increase production.

_____ 7. Steam-powered factories made more luxuries and goods available to everyone.

_____ 8. Workers had to accept the wages (money) that the factory owner determined.

_____ 9. Steam-powered mills did not produce pollution.

_____ 10. Working conditions became worse for many people.

_____ 11. The pollution from steam-powered factories caused health problems.

_____ 12. Machines replaced craftsmen and women.

_____ 13. Steam locomotives and steamboats made it easier to transport people and goods.

_____ 14. The amount of crime did not increase in large cities.

15. Choose one of the power statements above. If the statement is true, write two or three sentences explaining why it is true. If the statement is false, write two or three sentences explaining why it is false.

_____

_____

_____

_____

Name: _____ Date: _____

Who Invented It?

Answer each question with a name from the box below.

Karl Benz	**W. H. Hoover**	**Rudolf Diesel**	**James Watt**
King Camp Gillette	**Henry Ford**	**Clarence Birdseye**	**Samuel Morse**
Alessandro Volta	**Isaac Singer**	**Alexander Graham Bell**	

1. Who invented a lightweight vacuum cleaner in 1908? _____

2. Who invented the safety razor? _____

3. Who invented Morse code? _____

4. The volt, which measures the strength of an electric current, is named after which Italian scientist? _____

5. Who invented modern frozen food? _____

6. Who set up a car company in America? _____

7. A telephone company was named after which inventor? _____

8. Who invented a practical sewing machine? _____

9. Who invented the diesel engine? _____

10. The watt, a unit that measures the rate at which electricity is generated, was named after which Scottish inventor? _____

11. Who was the first person to build and run a gasoline-driven car? _____

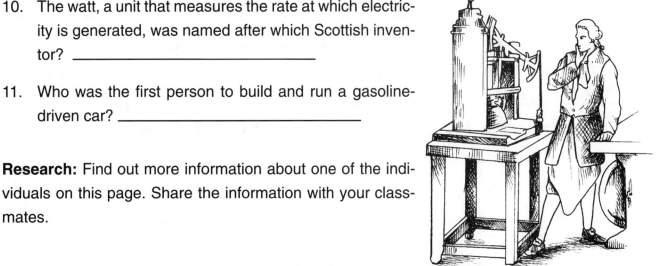

Research: Find out more information about one of the individuals on this page. Share the information with your classmates.

Name: _____ Date: _____

Interview an Inventor

Which inventor fascinated you the most? Samuel Morse? Robert Fulton? Eli Whitney? Henry Ford? Elisha Otis? Orville or Wilbur Wright? Thomas Edison? Michael Faraday? James Watt? Alexander Graham Bell? Choose one of these inventors or select an inventor of your choice.

Imagine that you have the opportunity to interview this inventor. Answer the questions below as that inventor might have done. Use this book, the Internet, or other reference sources if you need help.

Inventor's name: _____

What was your childhood like? _____

_____

_____

_____

How did you get interested in inventing things? _____

_____

_____

_____

Please describe your invention. _____

_____

_____

_____

What was the most frustrating thing that happened as you worked on your invention?

_____

_____

Who helped you in some way? _____

_____

Do you think your invention has changed our country or the world? In what way?

_____

_____

_____

Name: _____ Date: _____

Cool Facts!

Team up with a partner to find the missing word in each cool fact below. Use the Internet and other reference sources if you need help.

1. Guglielmo Marconi invented the "wireless" that used radio waves. When he died in 1937, the world's radio stations were silent for _____ minutes in his honor.

2. The Erie Canal was _____ miles long.

3. The British government once worried that passengers traveling more than _____ miles per hour on a steam locomotive might suffocate!

4. Many elevators still use the _____ name, which is the last name of the inventor of the safety elevator.

5. _____ was the first woman doctor of science in Europe. She was also the first woman to receive the Nobel Prize and the first person to receive the Nobel Prize twice.

6. When he was making a model of his first steam engine, _____ stole a thimble from his wife's sewing basket. He used the thimble to make a vital stop for the end of a pipe.

7. The first food cans had to be opened with a _____ and chisel!

8. Over _____ Model T's were made in 1922.

9. The first _____ sets had screens that were only about the size of a post-card.

10. Until the 1960s, television pictures were transmitted in _____ only.

11. In 1901, Hubert Booth, a Scotsman, invented an electric machine that sucked in dust. It was so _____ that it had to be pulled from house to house by horses.

12. Henry Ford introduced the Model T in 1908. The only color it came in was _____ because this color dried more quickly.

13. In 1824, a can of roast veal was taken along on an expedition to the Arctic. The can was opened in _____, a hundred and fourteen years later. The veal was in perfect condition.

57

Name: _____ Date: _____

Reflecting on Industrialization

Answer the following questions. Use your own paper if you need more room.

1. As you have learned in this book, industrialization provided great benefits for people. Those benefits have made our lives easier and healthier than those of Americans who lived 200 years ago. What are 10 benefits of industrialization in your life?

   _____

   _____

   _____

   _____

   _____

2. Of course, those benefits came at a price. In the past, men, women, and children worked 16 hours or more a day, six days a week. They had to accept the low wages given by factory owners. The factories were not clean, and the machines were often dangerous. Industrialization has also caused pollution of the air and water. Many people today experience a stressful, fast-paced lifestyle because of industrialism. When you think about all the hardships that industrialization caused and continues to cause, do you think it was and still is a good thing for the world? Why or why not?

   _____

   _____

   _____

   _____

   _____

3. In what way does industrialization continue into the present? Do you think computers represent a new Industrial Revolution? Are there other areas in which a "revolution" might take place? What changes do you predict industrialization will bring to the future? What will be some benefits? What problems will it cause? Use the lines below to reflect on the future of industrialization.

   _____

   _____

   _____

   _____

   _____

Suggested Reading

Eli Whitney by Judith Alter. New York: Franklin Watts, 1990.

The Rise of Industry 1860–1900 by Christopher Collier and James Lincoln Collier. New York: Benchmark Books, Marshall Cavendish, 2000.

The Industrial Revolution by James A. Corrick. San Diego, California: Lucent Books, 1998.

Discovery and Inventions by Geoff Endacott. New York: Viking, 1991.

Samuel Morse by Mona Kerby. New York: Franklin Watts, 1991.

The Inventor Through History by Peter Lafferty and Julian Rowe. New York: Thomson Learning, 1993.

Robert Fulton by Elaine Landau. New York: Franklin Watts, 1991.

53½ Things That Changed the World and Some That Didn't by Steve Parker. Connecticut: The Millford Press, 1995.

Thomas Edison and Electricity by Steve Parker. New York: Chelsea House Publishers, 1992.

The Usborne Book of Inventors by Struan Reid and Patricia Fara. London: Usborne Publishing Ltd., 1994.

Inventors and Ingenious Ideas by Peter Turvey. New York: Franklin Watts, 1992.

The Industrial Revolution by Philip Wilkinson and Michael Pollard. New York: Chelsea House Publishers, 1995.

Turning Points in History: Scientists Who Changed the World by Philip Wilkinson and Michael Pollard. New York: Chelsea House Publishers, 1994.

Answer Keys

Industrialization (p. 3)
1. Muscle, wind, water
2. It was fueled by coal.
3. No. The changeover from human power to machine power was a gradual process.

What Is a Machine? (p. 4)
7. Industry: manufacturing companies and other businesses taken together.
8. Wind: windmills; water: waterwheels

Water Power (p. 5)
A. sluice
B. buckets
C. grinding stones
D. stream
E. wheel
F. shaft
G. gears
H. flour

Standardized Parts (p. 8)
4. Uniformity: not being different in any way; all alike
   Interchangeable: easily switched with something else
5. Standardized parts increased production.

Eli Whitney's Solutions (p. 9)
1. Solution: Use interchangeable parts.
2. Problem: The country lacked skilled gunsmiths.
   Solution: Design machines that unskilled workers could use.
3. Problem: People doubted that interchangeable parts would work.
   Solution: Whitney gave a demonstration that proved his idea worked.

Learning Textile Terms (p. 10)
1. Waterwheel: a large wheel that is turned by water flowing over or under it. Waterwheels are used to provide power.
2. Mill: a large factory with machinery for processing textiles, wood, paper, steel, etc.
3. Textile: a fabric or cloth that has been woven or knitted.
4. Loom: a machine used for weaving cloth.
5. Weave: to make cloth by passing threads or strips over and under each other.
6. Spin: to make thread by twisting fine fibers together.

How Do You Make Clothes? (p. 11)
6. 6, 1, 3, 2, 5, 4

The Effects of Eli Whitney's Cotton Gin (p. 12)
Any five of these effects: Growing cotton became profitable. Plantation owners wanted more slaves. Many people found jobs ginning cotton. People paid debts and land increased in value. Factories in the North started to use cotton to make cloth. The shipping industry grew.

Depending on Credits (p. 15)
1. If there were many children available to work in his mill, he would probably not treat them well. If they didn't work as hard as he wanted them to, he would just get other children to work for him.
2. If there were only a few children available to work in his mill, he might treat them a little nicer because he needed them to stay and work for him.
3. The factory workers didn't have money to spend at other places. They could only buy things at the company store.
4. Some factory owners raised prices because they knew their company store was the only place the workers could purchase things.

Learning Steam Power Terms (p. 18)
1. Steam: the vapor that is formed when water boils
2. Condenser: an apparatus in which steam is condensed back into water
3. Boiler: a tank that is heated to turn water into steam
4. Engine: a machine that changes an energy source into movement.
5. Piston: a disk or cylinder that moves back and forth in a large cylinder; Steam engines have pistons. Their back-and-forth movement is converted to rotational movement.
6. Rotary motion: turning on an axis like a wheel
7. Governor: an attachment to a machine for automatic control or limitation of speed

The First True Steam Engine (p. 19)
1. The lid will move.
   A. Wooden rocking beam
   B. Connecting chain
   C. Cylinder
   D. Boiler
   E. Fire
   F. Pump rods
   G. Mine shaft

Water Power vs. Steam Power (p. 21)
1. No   2. No   3. Yes   4. Yes
5. Yes   6. Yes   7. No   8. Yes
9. No   10. Yes   11. Yes

60

Robert Fulton (p. 22)

1. The family had to sell the farm. Robert Fulton, Sr., died.
2. Fulton invented things that he thought were necessary.
3. Artistic: Fulton was an accomplished painter. Thoughtful: He bought a farm for his mother that had a flower garden. Answers will vary.

Robert Fulton (cont.) (p. 23)

5. There were too many struggling painters in Europe. It was an exciting time for inventors because the Industrial Revolution was underway.
6. The British government wanted to control the market for all the goods that could be made with steam engines.

Canals (p. 25)

1. Canal: a channel for water that is dug across land
2. Canals were built to connect bodies of water so that barges or ships could travel between them.
3. As the horses walked a path running alongside the canal, they towed freight and passenger barges.
4. Horses
5. The hoggees were the men who drove the teams that pulled the canal boats.
6. A cobbler is someone who makes or repairs shoes.
7. Hoggees would wear out their shoes as they walked along the canal.
8. Canals and rivers often froze until spring.
9. Most roads then were unpaved and muddy.
10. A lock is a part of a canal with gates at each end where boats are raised or lowered to different water levels.

The Erie Canal (p. 26)

Teacher check map.

Fascinating Facts About the Erie Canal (p. 27)

1. 1817
2. farmers
3. Ireland
4. one dollar
5. 85
6. Lake Erie
7. eastern
8. cities
9. Mills
10. immigration
11. west
12. Freight
13. Buffalo
14. deep
15. wide
16. tolls
17. thousands
18. hoggees
19. hostellers
20. steam trains

All About Iron (p. 30)

1. Stone, bone, wood, bronze
2. They would fall apart, bend, or break.
3. Iron tools were hard and would last.
4. Iron ore is a natural rock that contains iron.
5. Iron
6. Large buildings

7. The machines were large and operated by belts from an overhead shaft. They needed huge, open floor areas for production and storage.

Taller and Taller Buildings (p. 31)

1. Crystal Palace
2. Eiffel Tower
3. Home Insurance Building
4. 52 stories
5. 1,250 feet or 381 meters
6. 1,454 feet or 443 meters
7. 1,821 feet or 550 meters

Inventing a Safe Elevator (p. 32)

1. New York City
2. standard-sized
3. mass-produced
4. hoists
5. cables
6. stairs
7. Otis
8. safety mechanism
9. elevator
10. World's Fair
11. cut
12. possible

How Did Steam Locomotives Affect America? (p. 34)

All answers +

Samuel Morse (p. 35)

1. Electricity and art
2. Inventing things
3. the semaphore telegraph system.

Samuel Morse (cont.) (p. 36)

4. electricity might be able to transmit messages.
5. he used ordinary materials.
6. He kept working on the telegraph and trying to interest others.

Samuel Morse (cont.) (p. 37)

7. his invention would be important someday.
8. stringing the wire from tall poles above the ground.

Morse Code (p. 38)

1. SOS; It is the International Distress Call.
2. Goodbye

Alike and Different (p. 39)

Samuel Morse only: early interest in electricity; born in 1791.
Robert Fulton only: early interest in finding new ways to complete tasks; born in 1765.
Both: invented several things; perseverant; studied art in Europe; experienced hardships.

Learning Electricity Terms (p. 41)

1. E
2. F
3. G
4. C
5. A
6. B
7. H
8. D

A History of Electricity (p. 42)
1. Lightning frightened many people.
2. The Netherlands is a small country in Europe.
3. Those sparks were amazing.
4. Electricity was an interesting subject.
5. I wonder why it took so long.
6. Edison also invented the phonograph.

How Does Electricity Affect the Earth? (p. 43)
1. coal	2. steam	3. generators
4. carbon dioxide		5. increasing
6. heat	7. greenhouse	8. reduce
9. fossil	10. energy	11. Nuclear
12. Ittireeciyc	13. electricity	

Thomas Edison Crossword Puzzle (p. 45)

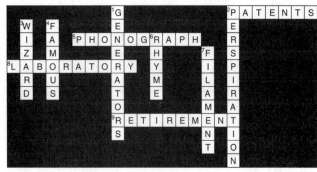

Hello, How Are You? (p. 46)
A. 2	B. 11	C. 7	D. 8	E. 6
F. 9	G. 5	H. 4	I. 1	J. 3
K. 10				

One Thing Affects Another (p. 47)
1. Effect: The coal industry boomed.
2. Cause: The coal industry needed trains and rails made of high quality steel. A technology that produced high quality steel became available.
3. Cause: There were many new railroads.
   Effect: The mail delivery was speeded up.
4. Effects: Americans could order products from distant cities. Newspapers could report news from across the nation. Railroad engineers could find out the exact locations of trains.

One Thing Affects Another (cont.) (p. 48)
5. Effect: Heinrich Hertz used Maxwell's information to build an electrical gadget that gave off invisible waves.
6. Cause: Guglielmo Marconi varied the waves so they could carry messages.
7. Effect: Home radios became common.
8. Cause: Scientists found ways to send pictures by radio waves.
   Effect: Vladimir Zworking devised the electronic television system.

Get the Message? (p. 49)
1. Smoke signals warned other Native Americans about the approach of the U.S. Cavalry.
2. What hath God wrought!
6. That's one small step for man, one giant leap for mankind.

Making Cars on an Assembly Line (p. 51)
5. Farmers could use the cars to get to town and to visit neighboring farmers.
6. The Model T could pass over bumpy dirt roads.

Before 1870 and After 1900 (p. 52)
1. 1870	2. 1900	3. 1900	4. 1870
5. 1870	6. 1900	7. 1870	8. 1900
9. 1870	10. 1870		

Industrial Mathematics (p. 53)
1. $\frac{1}{4}$	2. $\frac{1}{2}$	3. 35 years	4. 360
5. 48,000	6. 580	7. 35,000	8. 18 years
9. $490	10. 719,000		

Power Statements (p. 54)
1. True	2. False	3. True	4. False
5. True	6. False	7. True	8. True
9. False	10. True	11. True	12. True
13. True	14. False		

Who Invented It? (p. 55)
1. W.H. Hoover	2. King Camp Gillette
3. Samuel Morse	4. Alessandro Volta
5. Clarence Birdseye	6. Henry Ford
7. Alexander Graham Bell	8. Isaac Singer
9. Rudolf Diesel	10. James Watt
11. Karl Benz	

Cool Facts! (p. 57)
1. two	2. 360
3. 12	4. Otis
5. Madam Curie	6. James Watt
7. hammer	8. one million
9. television	10. black and white
11. big	12. black
13. 1938	